W9-AYO-249

**DATE DUE**

| | | | |
|---|---|---|---|
| MAY 25 1984 | | | |
| JUN. 20 1984 | | | |
| AUG. 23 1984 | | | |
| OCT. 1 6 1984 | | | |
| NY 24 OC 31'09 | | | |
| FE 26'93 NO 02 10 | | | |
| MR 15'93 | | | |
| AP 29'93 | | | |
| DEC 15 '93 | | | |
| OC 03'05 | | | |
| OC 18 05 | | | |
| | | | |

J
641.59

**Weston, Reiko**
**Cooking the Japanese way**

EAU CLAIRE DISTRICT LIBRARY

# cooking the JAPANESE way

Seated on floor cushions at a traditional low Japanese table, these diners are enjoying *sukiyaki* that was cooked at their table. (Recipe on page 28.)

# cooking the JAPANESE way

REIKO WESTON

EAU CLAIRE DISTRICT LIBRARY

80843

easy menu *ethnic* cookbooks

Lerner Publications Company ■ Minneapolis

5/5/84 Main line 7 95

**Series Editor: Patricia A. Grotts**
**Series Consultant: Ann L. Burckhardt**
**Special Consultant: Kay Kushino**

**Photographs by Robert L. and Diane Wolfe**
**Drawings and Map by Jeanette Swofford**

The page border for this book is based on a Japanese rice symbol.

*To boys and girls around the world*

Copyright © 1983 by Lerner Publications Company

All rights reserved. International copyright secured.
No part of this book may be reproduced in any form whatsoever
without permission in writing from the publisher except for
the inclusion of brief quotations in an acknowledged review.

Library of Congress Cataloging in Publication Data

Weston, Reiko.
  Cooking the Japanese way.

  (Easy menu ethnic cookbooks)
  Includes index.
  Summary: An introduction to the cooking of Japan
featuring basic recipes for soups, appetizers,
main dishes, side dishes, and desserts. Also
describes some special ingredients used in Japanese
dishes, how to set a Japanese table, and how to
eat with chopsticks.
    1. Cookery, Japanese—Juvenile literature.
2. Japan—Juvenile literature. |1. Cookery,
Japanese| I. Wolfe, Robert L., ill.  II. Swofford,
Jeanette, ill.  III. Title.  IV. Series.
TX724.5.J3W47   1983      641.5952      82-12656
ISBN 0-8225-0905-9 (lib. bdg.)

Manufactured in the United States of America

1  2  3  4  5  6  7  8  9  10  91  90  89  88  87  86  85  84  83

# CONTENTS

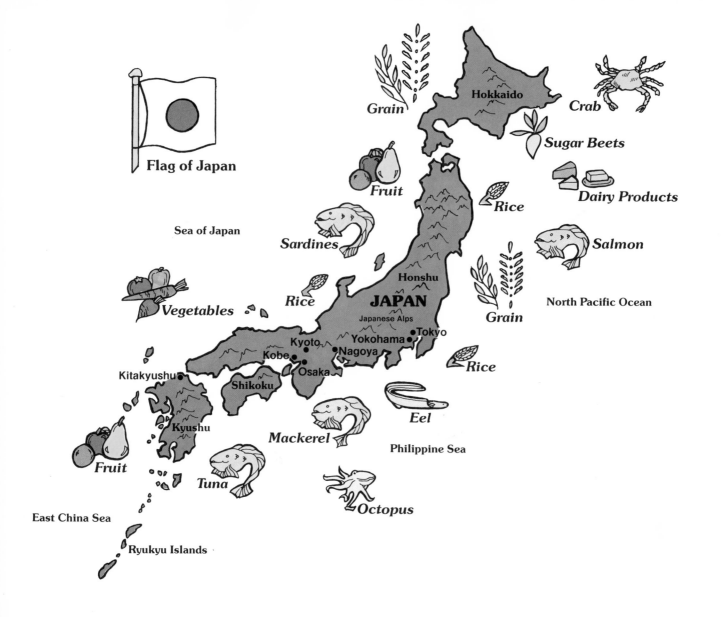

Flag of Japan

Grain

Hokkaido

Crab

Sugar Beets

Dairy Products

Fruit

Rice

Sea of Japan

Sardines

Salmon

Rice

Honshu

JAPAN

North Pacific Ocean

Japanese Alps

Grain

Vegetables

Rice

Kyoto

Yokohama

Tokyo

Kobe

Nagoya

Osaka

Kitakyushu

Rice

Shikoku

Kyushu

Eel

Mackerel

Fruit

Philippine Sea

Tuna

Octopus

East China Sea

Ryukyu Islands

# INTRODUCTION

Today the nation of Japan is known around the world as a producer of efficient, well-made automobiles, televisions, cameras, computers, and thousands of other useful machines and gadgets. Although Japanese technology is famous, other aspects of Japanese life may not be as well known to people in other parts of the world. Japan is a modern industrial giant, but it is also a country proud of its ancient cultural traditions. A distinctive style of cooking is one very important tradition that lives on in modern Japan.

Like the cooking of other countries with a long history, Japanese cooking has grown and changed over the more than 2,000 years that Japan has existed. Important developments in Japanese history such as the first contact with Europeans in the 1500s brought new foods and new cooking methods into Japanese life. Despite these changes, the basic elements of Japanese cooking have remained the same for a very long time.

## FRESH IS BEST

Today as in the past, one of the most important characteristics of Japanese cooking is that it uses only the freshest kinds of foods. Japanese cooks usually shop every day, buying food to be prepared for that day's meals. This emphasis on fresh food is part of the deep respect for nature that is so important in Japanese culture. The Japanese believe that the products of the earth and the sea should be used in ways that preserve their natural forms and flavors as much as possible.

When they plan meals during the year, Japanese cooks try to use the fruits and vegetables that grow in that particular season. In spring, wild plants such as *warabi* (fern shoots) and *seri* (watercress) can be gathered

The freshest available vegetables are used in Japanese cooking. This assortment of familiar and less familiar vegetables includes carrots, green and white onions, bamboo, broccoli, *daikon,* and white and black mushrooms.

in woodlands and forests. Summer brings the ripening of such familiar garden vegetables as tomatoes, lettuce, cucumbers, eggplants, beans, and peas. In the autumn, a wild mushroom harvest takes place when the large *matsutake* appears in pine forests. Winter meals feature root vegetables like carrots and turnips as well as *daikon,* a large white radish, and the root of the burdock, a plant considered a weed in the United States.

At any time of the year, Japanese cooks can get fresh fish taken from the waters that surround the island nation. Fish markets display tuna, sea bass, yellowtail, and cod along with other products of the sea such as octopus, sea urchin, and many delicious kinds of edible seaweed. Excellent beef, pork, and chicken are also available and appear frequently on a Japanese menu.

## JAPANESE STAPLES

In addition to the freshest vegetables, fish, or meat, several kinds of staple food are important in Japanese cooking. The most

important is of course rice. No Japanese meal would be complete without small bowls of boiled or steamed rice to accompany the other dishes. In fact, the word for rice—*gohan*—is also the word for food in the Japanese language. Today many Japanese families use electric rice cookers to be sure that this vital part of the meal is prepared perfectly every time.

Japanese people eat noodles almost as often as they eat rice, and they can choose from a great variety. Brown noodles called *soba,* made from buckwheat flour, are perhaps the most common. *Udon* and *somen,* two kinds of wheat-flour noodles, are also very popular. Noodles are served hot or cold, and they are

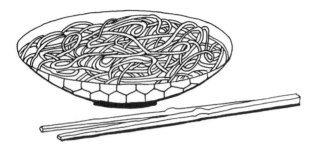

so much a part of the Japanese diet that they are even eaten for a quick snack in the way that an American might eat a sandwich or an apple.

Soybean products are another staple of the Japanese diet. It would be difficult to cook a Japanese meal without soy sauce, which is used as commonly as Westerners use salt. Two other soy products are *miso,* a soybean paste used in soups and other dishes, and *tofu,* a custard-like substance made of soybean curd. Japanese cooks serve *tofu* by itself and also use it as an ingredient in many dishes. This unique soybean product is now available in North America and has become popular as a meatless source of protein.

## COOKING THE JAPANESE WAY

When they prepare food, the Japanese use basic cooking methods that preserve or enhance the natural flavors of all the ingredients. Most of these methods are simple and easy, but they produce dishes that taste delicious and are beautiful to see.

One of the most common styles of Japanese cooking is called *nimono.* This category includes dishes that are made by gently boiling or simmering ingredients such as fish, meat, or vegetables in a seasoned broth. *Yakimono* is food prepared by broiling, usually over a charcoal fire. The famous Japanese *tempura*—food deep-fried in batter —belongs to the general group of *agemono,* or fried things.

A special category of Japanese cooking is *nabemono,* hearty one-pot dishes that are usually cooked at the table and include meat, fish, vegetables, tofu, and perhaps some noodles. *Aemono* dishes are made up of cooked vegetables and seafood that are served cold and tossed with various sauces;

*sunomono* dishes have vinegar dressings; *ohitashi* are boiled green vegetables, topped with *katsuobushi* (dried *bonito* fish shavings) or sesame seeds and served with soy sauce. *Tsukemono* are the many pickled vegetables that are served with most Japanese meals.

When Japanese cooks plan a meal, they choose different dishes from these and other basic cooking categories. Rather than the salad, main course, and side dishes that are common in Western meals, a Japanese meal consists of foods prepared in different ways or with contrasting flavors. A sharp-tasting *sunomono* dish might be served with *teriyaki,* a broiled food with a sweet sauce. Crunchy *tsukemono* makes a good contrast with a *nabemono* brimming with meat or seafood and vegetables.

The recipes in this book are divided into groups based on the style of cooking or preparation they require. You will be able to plan meals in the Japanese style by choosing dishes from these basic categories.

## A TREAT FOR THE EYES

In choosing and preparing dishes for a meal, Japanese cooks think not only of the food's freshness and flavor but also of its appearance. They believe that good food should appeal to the mind and the eye as well as to the taste buds. Therefore they try to make sure that the colors of the various ingredients and dishes in a meal look well together. Many cooks use special methods of cutting and arranging ingredients. Finally they serve food in well-designed bowls, plates, and cups that make an appropriate background for its color and texture.

In Japan, cooking and serving food is considered an art. But it is an art that is an essential part of everyday life. Japanese women preparing meals for their families rely on the same principles of freshness, simplicity, and beauty as cooks do in the finest restaurants. When you try the recipes in this book, think of yourself as an artist using vegetables, fish, and meat to make something that is both delicious and beautiful. Then you will really be cooking the Japanese way.

# TYPICAL JAPANESE MEALS

Although today some people in Japan have Western-style meals, many still eat traditional foods. For example, a family might sit down to a breakfast of bean paste soup, seaweed, a coddled or soft-boiled egg, rice, pickles, and tea. A summer lunch might be cold noodles, cooked vegetables, and tea. And a typical evening meal might include a *nabemono* dish with tofu, vegetables fixed with a sauce, and of course tea. The Japanese seldom eat sweet desserts, but fresh fruit is often served at the end of a meal.

You can put together your own Japanese meals by choosing dishes from the groups shown below. You might want to try one of the typical Japanese meals or come up with your own combinations. Remember that the only rule is to combine dishes that have different flavors and yet go well together.

| *English* | *Japanese* | *Pronunciation Guide* |
| --- | --- | --- |
| STAPLES | SHŪ-SHO-KU | shoo-sho-koo |
| Rice | Gohan | go-hahn |
| Noodles | Menrui | mehn-roo-ee |
| Tea | Ocha | o-cha |
| SOUP | SHIRUMONO | shee-roo-moh-no |
| Clear soup | O-sumashi | oh-soo-mah-shee |
| Eggdrop soup | Tamago toji | tah-mah-goh toh-jee |
| Bean paste soup | Misoshiru | mee-soh-shee-roo |

| English | Japanese | Pronunciation Guide |
|---|---|---|
| DISHES WITH SAUCES | SUNOMONO/AEMONO | soo-no-moh-no/ah-ay-moh-no |
| Sesame seed dressing with broccoli | Goma-ae | goh-mah-ah-ee |
| Cucumber with crab | Kani to kyuri no sunomono | kah-nee toh kyoori no soo-no-moh-no |
| Spinach | Horenso | hor-rehn-so |
| ONE-POT DISHES | NABEMONO | nah-bay-moh-no |
| Simmered beef and vegetables | Sukiyaki | soo-kee-yah-kee |
| Chicken in a pot | Tori no mizutaki | toree no mee-zoo-tah-kee |
| BROILED DISHES | YAKIMONO | yah-kee-moh-no |
| Broiled chicken | Teriyaki | teh-ree-yah-kee |
| Shrimp and vegetables broiled on skewers | Kushiyaki | kuh-shee-yah-kee |
| Salt-broiled fish | Shioyaki | shee-oh-yah-kee |
| STEAMED DISHES | MUSHIMONO | moo-shee-moh-no |
| Eggs steamed in cups | Chawan mushi | chah-wahn moo-shee |

# BEFORE YOU BEGIN

Cooking any dish, plain or fancy, is easier and more fun if you are familiar with its ingredients. Japanese cooking makes use of some ingredients that you may not know. Sometimes special cookware is used, too, although the recipes in this book can easily be prepared with ordinary utensils and pans.

*Before* you start cooking, carefully study the following "dictionary" of terms and special ingredients. Then read through the recipe you want to try from beginning to end. Now you are ready to shop for ingredients and to organize the cookware you will need. Once you have assembled everything, you can begin to cook. Before you start, it is also very important to read *The Careful Cook* on page 43.

## COOKING UTENSILS

*charcoal grill* — A cooker in which charcoal provides the source of heat and food is placed on a grill above the coals

*colander* — A bowl-shaped dish with holes in it that is used for washing or draining food

*skewer* — A stick used to hold small pieces of meat, fish, or vegetables for broiling. The Japanese use bamboo sticks as skewers.

*steamer* — A cooking utensil designed for cooking food with steam. Japanese steamers have grates or racks for holding the food and tight-fitting lids. In Western cooking, vegetables are often steamed in a basket that fits inside a saucepan.

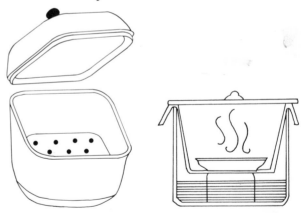

**Left:** A typical Japanese steamer. **Right:** This improvised steamer was made by placing a plate on top of an upside-down heatproof bowl or tin inside of a covered cooking pot.

## COOKING TERMS

*baste* — To pour or spoon liquid over food as it roasts in order to flavor and moisten it

*boil* — To heat a liquid over high heat until bubbles form and rise rapidly to the surface

*bone* — To remove the bones from meat or fish

*broil* — To cook directly under a heat source so that the side of the food facing the heat cooks rapidly

*brown* — To cook food quickly in fat over high heat so that the surface turns an even brown

*dice* — To chop food into small square-shaped pieces

*grate* — To cut into tiny pieces by rubbing the food against a grater; to shred

*marinate* — To soak food in a liquid in order to add flavor and to tenderize it

*preheat* — To allow an oven to warm up to a certain temperature before putting food in it

*sauté* — To fry quickly over high heat in oil or fat, stirring or turning the food to prevent burning

*simmer* — To cook over low heat in liquid kept just below its boiling point. Bubbles may occasionally rise to the surface.

## SPECIAL INGREDIENTS

*bamboo shoots* — Tender, fleshy yellow sprouts from bamboo canes. They can be bought fresh in Japan, but only canned ones are usually available elsewhere.

*chives* — A member of the onion family whose thin, green stalks are chopped and used to garnish many dishes

*dashinomoto* — An instant powdered soup base made from dried seaweed and flakes of dried *bonito* fish called *katsuobushi*. (Home-made soup stock is called *dashi*.)

*ginger root* — A knobby, light brown root used to flavor food. To use fresh ginger root, slice or grate off the amount called for and freeze the rest. Fresh ginger has a very zippy taste, so use it sparingly. (Don't substitute dried ground ginger in a recipe calling for fresh ginger, as the taste is very different.)

*katsuobushi* — Dried shavings of the *bonito* fish; used as a garnish for many cooked vegetable and other dishes and to flavor soup stock

*miso* — A paste made from soybeans used in soups, sauces, and as a garnish

*noodles* — An important staple that is available in many forms and served many ways. Three popular kinds are *soba* (buckwheat noodles), *somen* (thin wheat noodles), and *udon* (thick wheat noodles).

*rice* — An important cereal grain that comes in three varieties. *Short grain rice,* the kind used in the recipes in this book, has short, thick grains that tend to stick together when cooked. *Sweet* or *glutinous rice* is used to make special dishes. *Long grain rice* is fluffy and absorbs more water than other types. It is not used in Japanese cooking.

*rice vinegar* — Vinegar made from rice

*scallions* — A variety of green onion

*sesame seeds* — Seeds from an herb grown in tropical countries. Sesame seeds are white or black in color and are often toasted and used either whole or crushed.

*shiitake* — Black mushrooms, either dried or fresh, used in Japanese cooking. Dried mushrooms must be rinsed in lukewarm water before cooking to make them tender.

*shirataki* — Yam noodles, available canned at most large supermarkets and at Oriental food shops

*soy sauce* — A sauce made from soybeans and other ingredients that is used to flavor Oriental cooking. Japanese soy sauce is recommended for the recipes in this book.

*tofu* — A processed curd made from soybeans

# JAPANESE STAPLES/
Shu-sho-ku

## Rice/
Gohan

*Rice is the staple food in Japan, and a typical Japanese meal always includes hot, steamed rice. There are several different Japanese words that mean "rice," but the most dignified is* gohan *or "honorable rice."*

*For a tasty variation of this recipe, just add 1 cup of frozen green peas at the end of Step 2 to make* mame gohan *(mah-may goh-hahn), or rice with green peas.*

**2 cups short-grain white rice, uncooked**
**2½ cups water**

1. Wash rice in a pan with cold water and drain in a colander.
2. In a covered heavy pot or saucepan, bring rice and water quickly to a boil. Lower heat and simmer until all water is absorbed (about 30 minutes).
3. Turn off heat and let rice steam itself for another 10 minutes.

*Serves 6 to 8*

**Cooked *soba* noodles with a dipping sauce and a garnish of red pepper flakes and chopped green onion. In the foreground *(back to front)* are uncooked *udon, soba,* and *somen,* three popular kinds of Japanese noodles.**

# Noodles/
## Menrui

*In Japan, noodles are eaten hot or cold, and they are served in many different ways. Here are general instructions for cooking any kind of Japanese noodles— soba, somen, or udon—and recipes for serving them hot or cold.*

### 8 ounces noodles, uncooked

1. Bring 6 cups of water to a boil. Add noodles and return water to a boil, stirring occasionally. Cook for about 20 minutes or until noodles are soft.
2. Drain noodles in a colander and rinse in cold water to stop cooking.
3. **For hot noodles:** Set noodles aside and prepare broth.
3. **For cold noodles:** Put noodles in refrigerator to cool and prepare dipping sauce.

### Broth

**3 cups water**
**1 tablespoon dashinomoto**
**4 tablespoons soy sauce**
**1 tablespoon sugar (or to taste)**

1. Combine all broth ingredients in a pan and bring to a boil. Add noodles and bring to a boil again to heat noodles.
2. Remove from heat and serve noodles with broth in 4 individual serving bowls.
3. Top noodles with chopped green onion or dried red pepper flakes, if desired.
*Serves 4*

### Dipping Sauce

**2 cups water**
**1 teaspoon dashinomoto**
**6 tablespoons soy sauce**
**2 teaspoons sugar (or to taste)**

1. Mix together all ingredients and pour into 4 small dishes for dipping.
2. Divide noodles into 4 individual serving bowls and garnish with sliced cucumber and mandarin oranges. Serve with dipping sauce. *Serves 4*

EAU CLAIRE DISTRICT LIBRARY

# Tea/
## Ocha

*Ever since the 9th century, the Japanese have been drinking tea. A filled teapot stands on Japanese tables during every meal. A cup of tea is also often enjoyed during any conversation, business or social. Although the Japanese do drink Western tea, Japanese loose green tea is still the most popular. It is always drunk plain, without milk, sugar, or lemon.*

1. In a teakettle or saucepan, heat water to boiling and cool for 5 minutes.
2. Measure loose tea into a teapot. Use 2 teaspoons for a small teapot and 2 tablespoons for a quart-sized pot.
3. Pour hot water into the teapot and let stand for a moment.
4. Pour tea into cups. (Do not add additional water to the teapot until more tea is desired. This preserves the fragrance of the liquid and prevents the tea from becoming bitter.)

# SOUP/
## Shirumono

Soup is an important part of most Japanese meals. Clear soup *(o-sumashi)* is usually served at the beginning of a meal. This delicately flavored soup can be varied by the addition of many different kinds of garnishes. The slightly thicker, sweeter soups flavored with red or white soybean paste *(misoshiru)* are generally served toward the end of a formal Japanese meal. Both kinds of soups can be made with *dashinomoto,* a powdered soup base available at Oriental food stores.

# Basic Clear Soup/
## O-sumashi

**3  cups water**
**1  heaping teaspoon dashinomoto**
**½  teaspoon salt**
**½  teaspoon soy sauce**
**4  mushroom slices for garnish**
    **chopped chives for garnish**

1. In a saucepan, bring water to a boil.
2. Stir in dashinomoto, salt, and soy sauce.
3. Remove immediately from heat. Pour into 4 small bowls and garnish each with a mushroom slice and a pinch of chives.

*Serves 4*

**These delicious soups** *(left to right)*—eggdrop, bean paste, and clear—are served in beautiful Japanese lacquer bowls.

# Eggdrop Soup/
## Tamago Toji

**1 egg**
**2 tablespoons scallions, finely
     chopped**
**3 cups basic clear soup (see recipe
     on page 21)**

1. Beat egg and scallions together in a
small bowl.
2. In a saucepan, bring basic clear soup to
a boil. Swirl egg mixture around the
inside of the pan in a small stream,
making a circle.
3. Remove soup from heat and pour into
4 small bowls to serve.

*Serves 4*

# Bean Paste Soup/
## Misoshiru

**3 cups water**
**2 tablespoons dashinomoto**
**½ cup miso**
**½ cup tofu, cubed**
**2 scallions, chopped into thin rounds
     for garnish**

1. In a saucepan, bring water to a boil and
stir in dashinomoto and miso.
2. Add tofu and bring mixture to a boil
again.
3. Remove from heat, pour into four small
bowls, and garnish with scallions.

*Serves 4*

# DISHES WITH SAUCES/
## Sunomono and Aemono

These two groups of Japanese dishes include vegetables and seafood mixed with various kinds of sauces. The ingredients may be raw or lightly cooked to preserve their natural colors and textures. Sauces for *sunomono* dishes always include vinegar, while *aemono* sauces are made from toasted sesame seeds, soy sauce, *miso,* and many other good things.

When planning a Japanese meal, you might think of *sunomono* as playing the same role as salads do in a Western meal. Their tangy dressings and crisp textures provide a good contrast to meat dishes. *Aemono* dishes such as *goma-ae* give a special taste to familiar green vegetables like broccoli, green beans, and spinach.

# Cucumber with Crab/
## Kani to Kyuri no Sunomono

*This refreshing combination of cucumber slices and crabmeat has a tart dressing made with vinegar. For variety, you could use shrimp or scallops in place of the crab. Or serve the cucumber alone with the* sunomono *dressing.*

**2 cucumbers**
**1 teaspoon salt**
**6 ounces (¾ cup) canned crab or frozen crab, thawed**

**Dressing**

**¼ cup rice vinegar**
**2 tablespoons sugar**
**¼ teaspoon soy sauce**

1. Thinly slice cucumbers, place in bowl, and sprinkle with salt. Let stand for 5 minutes, then use your hands to gently squeeze water out of cucumbers.
2. Break up crab in small pieces.
3. In another bowl, combine vinegar, sugar, and soy sauce.
4. Put cucumber and crab in 4 small bowls and pour on dressing. Sprinkle with sesame seeds, if desired.

*Serves 4*

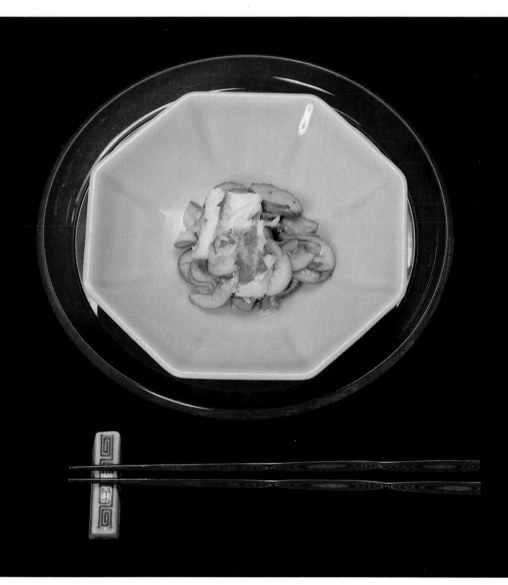

# Sesame Seed Dressing with Broccoli/ Goma-ae

*Goma-ae (sesame seed dressing) and broccoli is served at room temperature, so it can be prepared ahead of time. This dish can be made with broccoli, spinach, green beans, cabbage, cauliflower, or any other fresh green vegetable you have on hand.*

**1  pound broccoli, cup up in small (1-
     to 2-inch) pieces. (Do not use
     tough ends of broccoli stalks.)**
**3  tablespoons sesame seeds**
**3  tablespoons soy sauce**
**1  tablespoon sugar**

1. Cook broccoli in steamer or in pan with ½ cup water for 5 to 7 minutes. (Be careful not to overcook. Broccoli should be bright green when done.) Drain and set aside.
2. Prepare sesame seeds by putting them in a covered, dry frying pan and toasting them over medium heat, shaking the pan constantly so that seeds do not burn. When seeds begin to pop, remove the pan from the heat. Crush seeds lightly with a rolling pin or in a blender.
3. To broccoli, add soy sauce with sugar and sesame seeds and mix well.

*Serves 4*

# Boiled Spinach/
Horenso

*Another category of vegetable dishes,* ohitashi, *are boiled greens served with soy sauce and topped with* katsuo-bushi *(dried* bonito *fish shavings) or toasted sesame seeds. Other vegetables, such as broccoli or green beans, may be substituted for spinach in this recipe.*

**1  pound spinach**
**2  to 4 teaspoons soy sauce**
**3  tablespoons katsuobushi or sesame**
    **seeds**

1. Wash spinach well and cook in steamer or in pan with ½ cup water for about 3 minutes. (Do not overcook. Spinach should be bright green when done.)
2. Drain spinach and set in cold water to stop cooking. Then with hands, squeeze out as much water as possible.
3. Cut spinach into 1- to 2-inch pieces and stand in 4 individual serving bowls.

4. Garnish with katsuobushi or toasted sesame seeds and pour soy sauce over spinach. (See page 26 for instructions for toasting.)

*Serves 4*

# ONE-POT DISHES/
## Nabemono

*Nabemono* dishes combine meat or seafood and vegetables in one pot to make a hearty and satisfying meal. In Japan, *nabe* cooking is done at the table, using a pot heated over a gas or charcoal burner. Meals featuring *nabemono* are particularly popular in the winter because the heat of the burner warms the room as well as cooking the food.

To make your *nabemono* dish, you can use an electric frying pan or casserole. If you want to cook at the table as the Japanese do, prepare your ingredients ahead of time and arrange them neatly on a platter. Then invite your family or friends to watch while you cook a delicious *sukiyaki* or *mizutaki*.

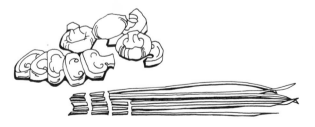

# Simmered Beef and Vegetables/
## Sukiyaki

*Sukiyaki is one of the most popular of the* nabemono *dishes. For a tasty variation on this one-pot dish, provide each diner with a beaten raw egg in a small bowl. Dip the meat and vegetables in the egg before eating. The heat from the food quickly cooks a coating of egg onto each piece, making everything taste even more delicious!*

1 to 1½ pounds rib-eye of beef
1 12-ounce block tofu, cut into 1-inch
   cubes
1 tablespoon oil
1 bunch (about 6) scallions, cut into
   2-inch pieces
1 small can shirataki
1 8-ounce can sliced bamboo shoots,
   rinsed under cold running water
1 cup (4 to 6) sliced fresh mushrooms
1 cup soy sauce (preferably Japanese)

**1½ cups water**
**3 tablespoons sugar**

1. Slice beef very thin. (If meat is slightly frozen, it is much easier to cut.)
2. Slice tofu into 1-inch pieces and set aside.
3. Heat oil in frying pan and sauté beef.
4. Add scallions, shirataki, bamboo shoots, mushrooms, and tofu.
5. Combine remaining ingredients to make a sauce. Pour sauce over meat and vegetables until they are half covered. Adjust heat so that sauce simmers.
6. After about 10 minutes, test a piece of meat to see if it is done.
7. Remove from pan and serve with hot rice.

*Serves 4*

*Sukiyaki* ingredients—beef, bamboo shoots, *shirataki,* scallions, tofu, and mushrooms—before and after cooking

*Mizutaki* is served with a dipping sauce and a garnish of lemon wedges, chives, and grated *daikon* with red pepper.

# Chicken in a Pot/ Mizutaki

*This simple chicken dish is served with a dipping sauce that adds a spicy taste. For color or garnish, you might want to add 1 cup of chopped carrots at the same time that you put in the cabbage. A similar dish prepared with beef is called* shabu shabu, *and when fish is used, it is called* chirinabe.

**1 chicken, cut up in serving pieces**
**2 cups water**
**2 cups Chinese cabbage, chopped**
**4 cups water**

1. Place chicken in cooking pot with 2 cups water and bring to a quick boil. Drain immediately. (If you are cooking at the table, this step should be done ahead of time.)
2. Add 4 cups fresh water and heat to simmering. Simmer for 20 minutes.
3. Add Chinese cabbage and cook for 10 more minutes.

4. Remove chicken and vegetables to individual serving plates. If desired, the remaining liquid may be served as soup. Season to taste with soy sauce.

## Dipping Sauce

**½ cup soy sauce**
**Juice of 1 lemon (about 3 table-spoons)**

## Garnish

**1 tablespoon chopped chives or scallions**
**½ tablespoon grated ginger root *or* grated radish and red pepper, mixed**

1. Mix soy sauce and lemon juice and pour into 4 small individual bowls.
2. Place garnishes in 4 small individual bowls.
3. Mix sauce and garnish to individual taste.
4. Dip chicken and vegetables in sauce before eating.

*Serves 4*

# BROILED DISHES/
## Yakimono

Many popular Japanese dishes are prepared by broiling. This method of cooking over high heat makes food crisp on the surface and tender and juicy inside. Meat, seafood, and vegetables are all delicious prepared as *yakimono.*

In Japan, "yaki" dishes may be cooked at the table on a small charcoal grill called a *hibachi. Hibachis* have also become popular in the United States and can be found in many specialty stores. If you can't get a *hibachi,* then a backyard barbecue grill or the broiler in your oven will work just as well. (When cooking with charcoal, it's a good idea to have an experienced cook help you to start the grill.)

# Broiled Chicken/
## Teriyaki

*One of the tastiest* yakimono *dishes is* teriyaki, *meat or seafood broiled with a sauce that gives it a shiny, glazed coating. This simplified recipe is baked in the oven instead of broiled as broiled food can burn easily. Beef, pork, shrimp, and some kinds of fish are also delicious prepared with* teriyaki *sauce.*

**½ cup soy sauce (preferably Japanese)**
**3 tablespoons sugar**
**1 teaspoon fresh ginger root, grated**
**3 tablespoons sesame seeds**
**a 1½- to 2-pound chicken, cut into**
**    small serving pieces**

1. Preheat oven to 375°.
2. Combine soy sauce, sugar, ginger root, and sesame seeds in a large bowl.
3. Place chicken in a baking dish and pour sauce over it. Bake for 45 minutes. Brush on more sauce as chicken bakes (about every 15 minutes).

*Serves 4*

*Tempura* onion rings and parsley provide a tasty accompaniment for *teriyaki* chicken.

**Many different ingredients may be used for *kushiyaki* including shrimp, scallops, chicken, beef, green onions, ginger root, and fresh mushrooms.**

# Shrimp and Vegetables Broiled on Skewers/ Kushiyaki

*Another popular category of* yakimono *is* kushiyaki, *foods broiled on skewers. (Kushi is the Japanese word for "skewer.") Like so many Japanese specialties,* kushiyaki *can be made with a combination of many different ingredients. Seafood, beef, pork, chicken, and vegetables such as mushrooms, onions, green pepper, and zucchini all make great* kushiyaki. *Use your imagination and pick your own favorites.*

**1 pound large fresh shrimp, peeled and deveined, or 2 7-ounce packages frozen peeled raw shrimp, thawed**
**¼ cup soy sauce**
**2 tablespoons sugar**
**1 tablespoon fresh ginger root, grated**
**1 green pepper**
**1 pound (2 cups) fresh whole mushrooms**

1. Combine soy sauce, sugar, and ginger root in a bowl.
2. Clean out and cut green pepper into 1-inch pieces. (Mushrooms may be broiled whole.)
3. Have an experienced cook start the charcoal grill, or preheat the oven to "broil."
4. Alternate shrimp, green pepper, and mushrooms on 12 small wooden skewers.
5. Broil skewered shrimp and vegetables for 6 to 10 minutes or until done. Dip the skewered shrimp and vegetables into sauce several times during broiling. Turn the skewers often so that all sides are broiled evenly.
6. Pour remaining sauce over skewers and serve with hot rice.

*Serves 4*

# Salt-Broiled Fish/ Shioyaki

*Salt-broiling is a simple but delicious way of preparing fish. The salt sprinkled on the fish before broiling causes a layer of fat under the skin to break down, giving it a special flavor. Any small whole fish may be cooked in this way. Fillets, or pieces of fish, may also be used as long as the skin has been left on.*

**2 whole trout, cleaned, or 1 pound
    fish fillets with skin on
  Salt**

1. Salt fish lightly on both sides and leave at room temperature for 30 minutes.
2. Start charcoal grill or preheat broiler.
3. Broil fish for about 5 minutes on each side or until golden brown.
4. Serve with soy sauce and lemon wedges.

*Serves 4*

**Sliced raw fish, or *sashimi,* is another very popular way of serving fish. Here red tuna and white squid are served with shredded lettuce, parsley, and ginger root.**

# STEAMED DISHES/
## Mushimono

The Japanese menu includes many dishes that are steamed, or cooked over boiling water. Most Japanese households have special utensils for steaming, with racks that hold food over the boiling water in the bottom of the container.

# Eggs Steamed in Cups/
## Chawan Mushi

*One of the most popular steamed dishes is* chawan mushi, *a tasty combination of egg custard, shrimp, and chicken. You might serve* chawan mushi *in place of soup at the beginning of a meal or as a light lunch accompanied by a vegetable dish. It is also delicious eaten cold.*

**6  small fresh shrimp, peeled and deveined, or 6 frozen peeled raw shrimp, thawed**
**4  eggs**
**1½ 15-ounce cans (about 3 cups) chicken broth or 3 cups basic clear soup (see recipe on page 21)**
**1½ teaspoons soy sauce**
**½  raw chicken breast, boned and diced**
**6  shiitake, softened in water (optional)**
**1  tablespoon chopped scallions**
**6  small pieces lemon peel**

1. In a bowl, beat eggs lightly and add chicken broth and soy sauce. Skim foam from surface with a spoon.
2. Divide chicken, shrimp, and mushrooms among 6 small heat-resistant cups.
3. Pour soup and egg mixture over meat and vegetables to cover.
4. Garnish each cup with a few scallions and a lemon peel.
5. If you have a steamer, steam the egg cups for 25 minutes over medium heat. If not, set the cups in a pan with about 1 inch of boiling water in it. Place the pan and cups in the oven and bake at 350° for 25 minutes.

*Serves 6*

# A JAPANESE TABLE

A traditional Japanese table is about the height of a coffee table and is used for most dinners. On formal occasions, however, each diner eats off a small lacquer tray with legs. The Japanese do not use chairs. Diners kneel on large flat cushions called *zabuton* (zah-boo-ton). Special guests are often seated before the *tokonoma* (toh-koh-noh-mah), or alcove, in which there is an arrangement of flowers, a decorative scroll, or some other art object.

Before the meal, each person is given a small, tightly rolled towel dampened with hot water. It is very refreshing, and not considered impolite, to bury your face in the towel before wiping your hands.

A Japanese table is set very simply. Large serving dishes are seldom used. Diners are served individual portions of food, each kind in its own separate china or lacquer bowl. The bowls are chosen to complement the shape and color of the food that they will hold.

Chopsticks are the primary eating utensils except when *chawan mushi* is on the menu. Then diners use flat china spoons to eat this egg custard dish. Soup is drunk straight from the bowl after the vegetables and other pieces of food contained in it have been eaten with chopsticks.

## EATING WITH CHOPSTICKS

Eating with chopsticks *(hashi)* means that table manners in Japan are different than those in countries where flatware is used. For example, it is good manners to pick up a rice bowl and hold it so that the food doesn't fall from the chopsticks to the table or into your lap. It is impolite, however, to use the "eating" ends of your chopsticks to help yourself from a *nabemono* pot. Instead, you should turn the chopsticks around to use the "clean" ends for dishing up. Sometimes special serving chopsticks are provided.

To Westerners, chopsticks seem to be very exotic eating utensils. But chopsticks are not difficult to manage once you have learned the basic technique. The key to using them is to

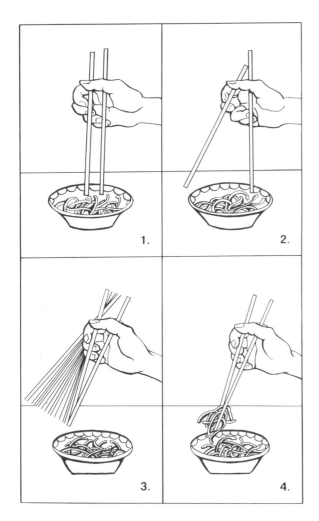

1.

2.

3.

4.

hold the inside stick still while moving the outside stick back and forth. The pair then act as pincers to pick up pieces of food.

Hold the thicker end of the first chopstick in the crook of your thumb, resting the lower part lightly against the inside of your ring finger.

Then put the second chopstick between the tips of your index and middle fingers and hold it with your thumb, much as you would hold a pencil.

Now you can make the outer chopstick move by bending your index and middle fingers toward the inside chopstick. The tips of the two sticks should come together like pincers when you bend your fingers. Once you get a feel for the technique, just keep practicing. Soon you'll be an expert!

# THE CAREFUL COOK

Whenever you cook, there are certain safety rules you must always keep in mind. Even experienced cooks follow these rules when they are in the kitchen.

1. Always wash your hands before handling food.
2. Thoroughly wash all raw vegetables and fruits to remove dirt, chemicals, and insecticides.
3. Use a cutting board when cutting up vegetables and fruits. Don't cut them up in your hand! And be sure to cut in a direction *away* from you and your fingers.
4. Long hair or loose clothing can easily catch fire if brought near the burners of a stove. If you have long hair, tie it back before you start cooking.
5. Turn all pot handles toward the back of the stove so that you will not catch your sleeve or jewelry on them. This is especially important when younger brothers and sisters are around. They could easily knock off a pot and get burned.

6. Always use a pot holder to steady hot pots or to take pans out of the oven. Don't use a wet cloth on a hot pan because the steam it produces could burn you.
7. Lift the lid of a steaming pot with the opening away from you so that you will not get burned.
8. If you get burned, hold the burn under cold running water. Do not put grease or butter on it. Cold water helps to take the heat out, but grease or butter will only keep it in.
9. If grease or cooking oil catches fire, throw baking soda or salt at the bottom of the flame to put it out. (Water will *not* put out a grease fire.) Call for help and try to turn all the stove burners to "off."

1. Rice
2. Noodles
3. Tea
4. Basic Clear Soup
5. Eggdrop Soup
6. Bean Paste Soup
7. Cucumber with Crab
8. Sesame Seed Dressing
   with Broccoli
9. Boiled Spinach
10. Simmered Beef and Vegetables
11. Chicken in a Pot
12. Broiled Chicken
13. Shrimp and Vegetables
    Broiled on Skewers
14. Salt-Broiled Fish
15. Eggs Steamed in Cups

1. 御飯
2. 麺類
3. お茶

4. お清汁の基本
5. 卵とじ
6. 味噌汁
7. 胡瓜と蟹の酢の物
8. ブロッコリの胡麻和え
9. ほうれん草のおひたし
10. すき焼
11. 鶏の水炊き
12. 鶏の照焼
13. 海老と野菜の串焼
14. 魚の塩焼
15. 茶碗蒸

## METRIC CONVERSION CHART

| WHEN YOU KNOW | MULTIPLY BY | TO FIND |
|---|---|---|
| MASS (weight) | | |
| ounces (oz) | 28.0 | grams (g) |
| pounds (lb) | 0.45 | kilograms (kg) |
| VOLUME | | |
| teaspoons (tsp) | 5.0 | milliliters (ml) |
| tablespoons (Tbsp) | 15.0 | milliliters |
| fluid ounces (oz) | 30.0 | milliliters |
| cup (c) | 0.24 | liters (l) |
| pint (pt) | 0.47 | liters |
| quart (qt) | 0.95 | liters |
| gallon (gal) | 3.8 | liters |
| TEMPERATURE | | |
| Fahrenheit (°F) temperature | 5/9 (after subtracting 32) | Celsius (°C) temperature |

## COMMON MEASURES AND THEIR EQUIVALENTS

3 teaspoons = 1 tablespoon

8 tablespoons = ½ cup

2 cups = 1 pint

2 pints = 1 quart

4 quarts = 1 gallon

16 ounces = 1 pound

# INDEX

*(recipes indicated by **bold face** type)*

## ABOUT THE AUTHOR

**Reiko Weston** came to Minneapolis from Tokyo, Japan, in 1953. She studied math at the University of Minnesota but interrupted her studies in 1959 to open a Japanese restaurant in downtown Minneapolis. Ten years later, Weston moved her successful restaurant business to a site on the Mississippi River, and it continues to be a popular eating place today. Since that time, she has opened two additional Japanese restaurants and a Chinese restaurant.

Weston was named Small Business Person of the Year in 1979 and was elected to the Minnesota Hall of Fame in 1980. Currently, she lives in Minneapolis with her two children. In addition to cooking, Weston enjoys reading and playing the harpsichord and the *koto,* a 13-string Japanese instrument.

# easy menu *ethnic* cookbooks

Cooking the **CHINESE** Way
Cooking the **ENGLISH** Way
Cooking the **FRENCH** Way
Cooking the **ITALIAN** Way
Cooking the **JAPANESE** Way
Cooking the **MEXICAN** Way
Cooking the **NORWEGIAN** Way
Cooking the **SPANISH** Way

**Lerner Publications Company**
241 First Avenue North, Minneapolis, Minnesota 55401